101 EXCUSES FOR NOT DOING HOMEWORK

Little, Carly.
  101 excuses for not doing homework.

  ISBN 0 86896 523 5.

  1. Homework — Humour — Juvenile literature.
  2. Wit and humour, Juvenile. I. Voutila, Ritva.
  II. Title. III. Title: One hundred and one
  excuses for not doing homework.

A828.302

First published in 1990 by Ashton Scholastic Pty Limited (Inc. in NSW), PO Box 579, Gosford 2250. Also in Brisbane, Melbourne, Adelaide, Perth and Auckland, NZ.

Typeset by Excel Imaging Pty Ltd, Sydney
Printed by Australian Print Group, Maryborough Vic.
Text set in Geneva

12 11 10 9 8 7 6 5 4   0 1 2 3 4 5 / 9

101 EXCUSES FOR NOT DOING HOMEWORK

Carly Little

illustrated by Ritva Voutila

ASHTON SCHOLASTIC
SYDNEY AUCKLAND NEW YORK TORONTO LONDON

But I didn't hear you set the homework!

A flash flood washed my homework away.

My dog had a heart attack and we had to
take him to the vet.

My sister hid it as a joke and won't tell me
where it is.

I was on the phone the whole time.

My cat died and I didn't have any paper to
wrap it in, so I used my homework pad.

I was doing my homework at the bank when
I was held-up by a robber who demanded it.

My mum was too sick to do it.

Dad ironed it.

My homework machine broke down.

My mum accidentally used it as a nappy
on my baby brother.

Dad gave me permission not to do
homework.

I was hungry so I ate it for a snack.

It got wet in last night's storm.

I watched television all afternoon.

I left it in the shower.

Not one pen in the house was working. I couldn't find a pencil and we don't have a typewriter, so I couldn't do it.

My girlfriend has it.

I went on a boat trip and it fell overboard.

I fed it to a horse which was dying of starvation.

I dropped it in the pool while teaching my brother how to swim.

I left it on the school bus.

My older sister forgot to finish it.

I got caught up in a parade.

The bird ate it.

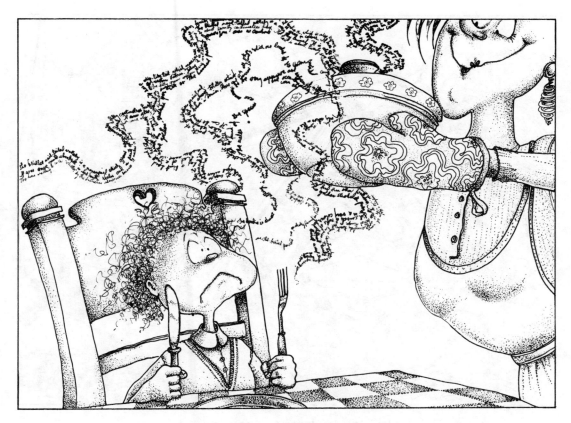

Mum stewed it for tea.

I left my book at school.

I felt sick.

I left it at my grandparents' house.

I accidentally flushed it down the toilet.

A chicken at my auntie's place took off
with it.

My dad thought it was scrap paper so he
threw it in the fire.

The dog ate it.

I was robbed last night and it's all they took.

The cat had kittens on it.

I had to go out with my friends.

My pet budgie escaped from its cage and
I had to catch it.

Next-door's pet tiger escaped and terrorised
the whole neighbourhood.

My sister in Grade 12 needed it for a test.

My cat buried it in its sandbox.

My schoolbag was full of papers, so I cleaned
it out and my homework went out too.

As I did it every night last week, I'm
having this week off.

It's in mum's car.

I showed you before. Remember!

A cricketing friend has it.

My uncle, Professor Brain, needed it for
an experiment.

It blew out of my hands.

The English teacher at high school has it.

I sent it to my penpal as a present.

My brother thought it was a tissue and
blew his nose on it.

I didn't have time to recharge my brain box.

Mum said I had to go to my grandparents'
house.

Friday afternoon shopping, Saturday a wedding, Sunday a barbecue.

Mum washed it and I forgot to take it off
the line.

I was hit on the toe with a cricket ball at
practice and so I didn't do it.

I went to a maths lesson all afternoon.

My next-door-neighbour's house burnt
down.

I bumped my head and went to bed.

I was kidnapped by Martians.

After school I did jobs for the principal and
then when I got home I had to go out.

I was held up on the way home.

There was a blackout and I couldn't find
my homework.

There was an all-night news program on television that was very educational, so I didn't do homework.

I left my bag on the UFO I was beamed up into
while walking home yesterday.

My brother dropped my homework over
the balcony.

I dropped it down a drain.

I left it at softball.

I spilt ink all over it.

Mum took it to work.

We were out all afternoon.

It's under my pillow.

I need a new book.

Someone borrowed it to copy out the answers.

I spilt chocolate syrup on it.

I had an attack of amnesia.

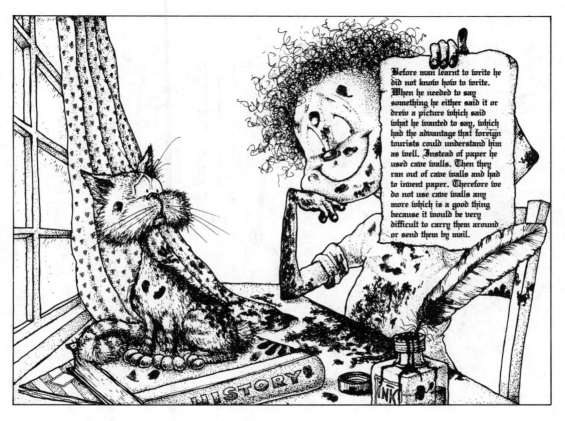

Another teacher bought it for twenty dollars
as an example of neatness.

I was doing it at my uncle's laboratory when
a robot went crazy and ripped it up.

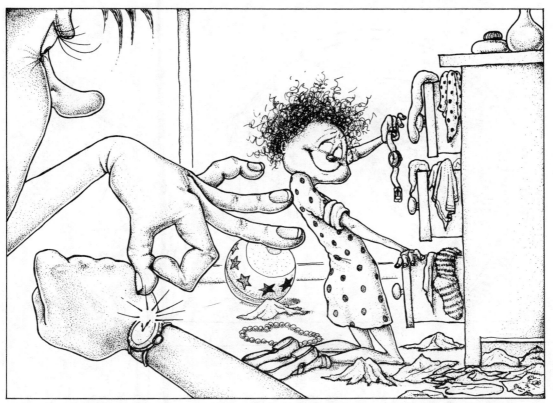

My Mickey Mouse watch said 7.00 pm when I started my homework but mum said to go to bed because it was 10.00 pm.

I did it but it's at home.

I lost my answer book.

It got stuck in the garbage disposal unit.

My dad put it in the safe and I've
forgotten the combination.

I lost my English workbook.

I couldn't write because my hand went to sleep.

My family are all sick and I have to look
after them.

I got hooked on a sad drama and was too
upset to do homework.

I had a headache, a sore throat, an aching tooth,
a swollen right hand and a sore toe.

I did it on a sheet of paper but I can't find
it now.

I'm so smart that I don't need to do homework.

My house was invaded by horrible monsters
who ate my homework book.

The dog buried it.

A strange vision told me to rip up my
homework.

My bag has a hole in it and it must have
fallen out.

I went shopping.

Mum needed it for a university
assignment.

I fell asleep on the toilet and forgot to do it.

Relations, whom I hadn't seen for twenty years,
arrived on our doorstep and we went out for tea.

Mum accidentally roasted it.

Porridge was spilt all over it.

My brother ripped it up.

I used the paper from my book for
origami.